Prickly and Smooth

by Rod Theodorou and Carole Telford

Contents

Heinemann

First published in Great Britain by Heinemann Library
an imprint of Heinemann Publishers (Oxford) Ltd
Halley Court, Jordan Hill, Oxford OX2 8EJ

MADRID ATHENS PARIS FLORENCE PRAGUE WARSAW
PORTSMOUTH NH CHICAGO SAO PAULO SINGAPORE TOKYO
MELBOURNE AUCKLAND IBADAN GABORONE JOHANNESBURG

Illustrations by Sheila Townsend and Trevor Dunton
Colour reproduction by Track QSP
Printed in China

99 98 97 96
10 9 8 7 6 5 4 3 2 1

ISBN 0 431 06397 4

British Library Cataloguing in Publication Data
Telford, Carole
  Prickly and Smooth. – (Animal Opposites Series)
  I. Title II. Theodorou, Rod III. Series
  591.1858

Photographic acknowledgements
Anthony Bannister/OSF p4; Christian Grzimek/Okapia/OSF p5; Vivek R Sinha/OSF p6 *top*; Daniel J Cox/OSF p6
bottom left; Alan Root/OSF p6 *bottom right*; David Curl/OSF p7 *top*; Tsuneo Nakamura/OSF p7 *bottom*;
Michael Fogden/OSF p8 *left*; Frank Schneidermeyer/OSF p8 *right*; Tui De Roy/OSF pp9, 17; Bob Bennett/OSF p10;
Stephen Dalton/OSF p11; Mike Kraetsch/OSF p12 *left*; Joe Mcdonald/OSF p12 *right*; G I Bernard/OSF pp13, 21
left; Robert Lubeck/OSF p14; Steve Turner/OSF p15; Partridge Films Ltd/OSF p16; Gregory K Scott/Photo
Researchers/OSF p18 *left*; Joan Root/OSF p18 *right*; Mark Jones/OSF p19; Leonard Lee Rue/Photo Researchers/OSF
p20; Mike Linley/OSF p21 *right*, back cover
Front cover: Alan Root/OSF *bottom*; Konrad Wothe/Bruce Coleman Ltd *top*

porcupine

hedgehog

sea urchin

Some animals are prickly.
Some animals are smooth.

snake

dolphin

tortoise

3

This is a porcupine.
Porcupines have prickles on
their backs.

This is a tortoise.
Tortoises have hard, smooth shells.

There are different kinds of porcupine. Some live on the ground and some live among the trees.

common porcupine

tree porcupine

North American porcupine

There are different kinds of tortoises. Some are small and some are huge.

7

Some porcupines live in rainforests or in hot deserts. Furry porcupines live in cold forests.

Tortoises always live in hot places.
If they get too cold they will die.

Porcupine prickles are called quills.
They are very sharp.

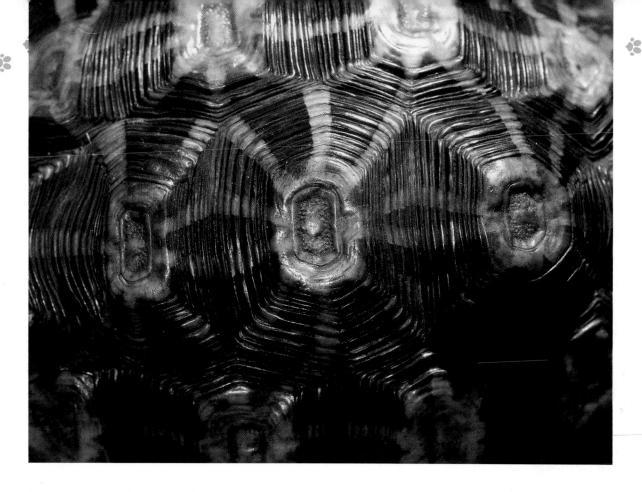

Tortoise shells are very hard.
They are very heavy, so tortoises
move very slowly.

Porcupines can lift up their quills.
This stops other animals eating them.

quills hidden

quills raised

Tortoises can pull their heads and legs into their shells.
They are safe from enemies in their hard shells.

Porcupines have long, sharp teeth. They have claws to help them climb.

Tortoises have thick, scaly skin.
They have a strong beak but no teeth.

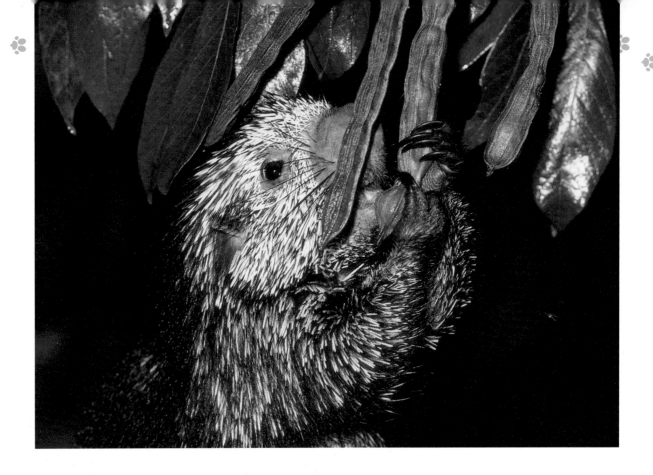

Porcupines eat leaves, berries and fruit.
They chew the bark off trees.

Tortoises eat fruit and plants.

Some porcupines make
a den to live in.
Sometimes they live
in caves.

Most tortoises do not need to make a nest.
They carry their homes on their backs!

Porcupines have two or three babies. The babies are covered in soft fur.

two-week old baby

Tortoises lay lots of eggs.
A baby tortoise
hatches out
of each egg.

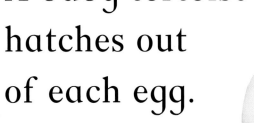

AMAZING FACTS!

Porcupines chew bones to sharpen their teeth.

A porcupine's teeth never stop growing!

Giant tortoises can live for over 100 years!

One giant tortoise can weigh as much as 4 people!

Index